INTRODUCTION

This book is the result of twenty years of research, both academic and in the field. The research that went into the topics covered here includes work with the leaders in the field of interest-based negotiation and decision-making at Harvard Law School. It also includes nearly two decades of practical experience as a negotiator in high stakes conflict around the world, from working with the Harvard Program on Negotiation facilitating dialogue among Israeli leaders over withdrawal from Gaza and West Bank settlements, to resolving labor conflict in India, to resolving litigation over educational segregation in the United States, to settling commercial litigation and business disputes in various industries, to negotiating joint ventures and other strategic business deals, to negotiating with key accounts.

Through all of these wide-ranging experiences, I have found some common principles that apply across the board. The real life examples chosen to illustrate the key points represent both specific situations in which people have handled challenges and typical situations that apply to many individuals and organizations.

Finally, the ideas in this book are infused with the varied experiences and perspectives of the thousands of business leaders, sales professionals, account managers, strategic supply chain managers,

John G. Shulman

business leaders, judges, lawyers, community leaders, activists and others I have had the great privilege of interacting with in negotiation and leadership workshops around the world. From the "win-win" relationship emphasis of the health care industry to the hard-edged negotiators in the transportation industry, I am constantly stretched and challenged to understand and interpret the many facets of human interaction. I thank all of the people who have so generously shared their ideas and challenged mine, so that we could all learn and grow in the process.

I hope you enjoy this book and find it useful. It is intended to be a practitioner's perspective on leadership and negotiation. While the theory underlying the topics covered is both sound and intriguing, this book is fundamentally written not from an academic perspective, but for those who do the heavy lifting – the field, the managers, the leaders – all on the front lines building relationships that can be leveraged in a sustainable manner to create value for their organizations.

Please feel free to contact me by phone (+1-866-987-9888) or email (jshulman@alignor.com) to share your ideas and perspectives on the topics covered in this book. I welcome your feedback and promise to take it into account in my future work!

TABLE OF CONTENTS

1. Selling Value
when all they want to talk about is price 7

2. Generating Consensus and Buy-in
with speed and flexibility 33

3. Handling Difficult People
without losing sleep or your shirt 45

CHAPTER **ONE**
Selling Value
when all they want to talk about is price

CHAPTER ONE
Selling Value

when all they want to talk about is price

The Challenge:

You know it when it happens. First, you get that sinking feeling. It's like being caught in whirlpool, going down into the sewer. Then you realize what it is: your buyer is stuck on price. Makes it seem like nothing else matters. "If we can only agree on price," she says—over and over again, like a broken record. You break out in a cold sweat. You'll never make your numbers if this deal falls apart. How can you get your buyer off price?

I call this situation "the price game." It comes in many forms. It is a game because the buyer wants to obtain all the value you can offer and then hammer you on price. The buyer's game is to "negotiate" price in isolation, out of the context of the rest of your deal. The seller may say something like, "Well, we have an agreement if you can just do something for me on the price." This game is of course the antithesis of selling value.

And sure, you want to sell "value," not price. But the reality is you need this deal. You need to bring home the bacon. You need to make your numbers this quarter. Problem is, the buyer's new.

She just got rotated in. She doesn't understand the importance of relationships. Not like the way it used to be, over a game of golf or breaking bread at a nice restaurant. Every time you say the word "value," she shoots back "price." Where do you go from here?

Bottom line: if you don't either get a better price from your finance team back at the home office (fat chance of that!), or get your buyer out of the price game, you might as well pack this one in. You need a strategic approach to handling the buyer's price game.

What we do when we're at our best:

Before we go any further, let's take a deep breath. Maybe a couple of them. Seriously. When the buyer starts harping on price, it can be helpful to take a deep breath or two so that you refrain from a knee-jerk reaction. You've got to stay strategic, which means you need to stay calm. Let your head, not your adrenal glands drive this deal.

Okay, now that you're calm, you're ready. You've got to understand the connection between controlling the negotiation process and influencing (though not necessarily "controlling") the outcome.[1] You see, the difficult buyer wants you to react emotionally to a provocation on price so that you betray weakness, or better yet, desperation, and fall

---

[1] While you can and should aspire to controlling the negotiation process, doing so will not guarantee that you can control the outcome of the negotiation. This is because you cannot control another person. By controlling the negotiation process, however, you gain your best shot at influencing the other person's behavior and decision-making.

into the price game. A calm, strategic approach will disarm all but the most obnoxious buyers and help you control the process.

Now that you're calm and strategic, what next? Is the problem solved? Not by a long shot. A deep breath may calm you down but doesn't—in itself—shift the buyer's focus from price to value. So how can you avoid the price game? Here are five proven strategies for selling value even when the buyer says the only thing that matters is price. (The five strategies should be utilized in the order they are presented below.)

> ### What we do when we're at our best:
>
> ***Strategy #1:*** *Put price in a broader context.*
>
> ***Strategy #2:*** *Consider other stakeholders.*
>
> ***Strategy #3:*** *Present the whole package.*
>
> ***Strategy #4:*** *Warn of consequences.*
>
> ***Strategy #5:*** *Reduce your package to meet the lower price.*

Strategy #1: Put price in a broader context.

When the buyer presses you about price, you cannot legitimately claim that price is irrelevant. It is relevant to the buyer. But it's also not the only thing relevant to her. Since price is a legitimate issue, go ahead and acknowledge that fact to the buyer up front. By acknowledging its importance, you are not agreeing to the buyer's demands on price. Nor are you communicating weakness or lack of conviction on your part. You are simply acknowledging that you have heard what your buyer is saying. You might say something like, "I hear you. I understand that price is really important to you."

This is your opportunity. And you have to move decisively and fast! By acknowledging that price is a legitimate issue, you have a fleeting opportunity to present something more favorable to you: value! So get to it! Don't waste the opportunity. Time for another deep breath. But make it a quick one!

Okay, price is not the only issue your account cares about.[2] Price is one of many issues—such as quality, terms, inventory management, total delivered cost, manufacturing efficiencies, switching costs, and many others—that your account cares about. **So once you've acknowledged your buyer's concern about price, negotiate for the opportunity to discuss with your buyer the other factors she should consider in addition to price.** Ask for 10 minutes or 5 minutes, or 2

---

[2] Of course, if price were in fact the only issue for your account, then you would be selling a perfectly fungible commodity and you would have a hard time staying out of the buyer's price game.

minutes. For example, you could say something like, *"Just to be sure our proposal meets your expectations and objectives, I'd like to confirm a few things. It will only take five minutes. Would that be okay?"*[3]

If she gives you permission to continue, which she should, you have to make the most of the opportunity. Go for the jugular! Actually, go straight to the critical interests of the buyer and her organization. Confirm that you are intent on satisfying their critical needs.

You can phrase your points in the form of questions, reminding your buyer that when she thinks of price (which you will get to in a moment), she should consider price in the context of how your entire solution will satisfy all of her organization's interests. In fact, to the extent your buyer represents not just her own interests but also the interests of an entire organization—which in the B2B context, she does—she must take not only her own narrow interests, such as lowering the price, into account but must also take into account the broader interests of other stakeholders in her organization, such as manufacturing, R&D and sales. In short, for your buyer, there are other issues to consider beyond price.

---

[3] *If the buyer objects to giving you, say, five minutes to confirm that your proposal will meet her objectives, she is most likely playing a game with you. Here, you should maintain your posture as a strategic negotiator and ask why she will not give you the five minutes. You might ask, "I appreciate that you don't have much time. Could I ask why you cannot spare five minutes for such an important decision?" If you do not get a satisfactory response, you might push a little harder, especially if there is a lot of money at stake. You could then say, "If you decide not to go with us after we've made our best proposal, I am comfortable with that. I would have some concerns, though, if you're unwilling to allow me five minutes to ensure that our proposal is indeed the best offer we can make."*

But it is not enough for you to think that. You have to be sure your buyer believes it. You have to communicate it. You might say something like, "Are you still looking for manufacturing process improvements and opportunities to reduce inventory?"

> Price is not the only issue your account cares about. **Price is one of many issues**—such as quality, terms, inventory management, total delivered cost, manufacturing efficiencies, switching costs, and many others—that your account cares about.

By acknowledging the importance of price to your buyer, you have negotiated for a precious opportunity to confirm with your buyer the importance of other issues beyond price. Don't squander it! And don't be misled by any apparent impatience your buyer may show or by her obsession with price. She _does_ care about things other than price!

Even if your buyer maintains a poker face, and refuses to "confirm" that anything other than price is important to her, she will give you cues that this price is not all she cares about. You should be able to read these cues in your buyer's body language, her facial expressions *and even her refraining from disagreeing w ith you.* What these things tell you is that you are making progress.

Your goal is simply to persuade your buyer to consider a variety of needs that will be satisfied if she accepts your proposal. Just don't expect her to acknowledge as much to your face. When you acknowledged the buyer's concern about price, you won an opportunity to make your case for value. You did not receive an invitation to try to convince your buyer that she was wrong, much less get her to admit this to you. At this point, all you can reasonably expect is an opportunity to make your case for value.

So what next? Make sure you're extremely specific in identifying your buyer's critical interests beyond price. You should identify not only her own interests but also the critical interests of her organization. You should remind the buyer in a friendly, professional, appropriate manner that she must consider a variety of factors other than price in order to make a sound purchasing decision. By putting price in this broader context of <u>all</u> of the account's critical interests, you de-emphasize price *as the determining factor* for the buyer's decision. You acknowledge that price is important to the buyer while showing that it is just one factor, among many, that she must consider.

While this may not in and of itself resolve the pricing game, it gets you off to a good start. And more often than you think, this sound foundation does indeed make the price conversation much easier when it occurs. Why does this happen? Because the more a buyer considers benefits other than a low price—such as high quality, unique features, superior customer service—the less important price becomes *as a percentage of the overall value your proposal brings to the buyer and her organization!*

Strategy #2: Consider other stakeholders.

Please do not misunderstand strategy #2. I am not advocating going around the buyer. You may have to do that eventually. But not yet. What I am saying is that you should figure out at this point who the other stakeholders in the buyer's organization are and what their interests are. That is crucial information.

When you are confronted by a buyer obsessed with price, particularly one who claims that "price is all that matters," you may be dealing with principal-agent divergence. Principal-agent divergence occurs when the buyer (the agent) has different interests from the organization (the principal) on whose behalf the agent is supposed to be negotiating. For example, your buyer may only care about price (because that is all she is evaluated on) while others in the organization, such as the VP of manufacturing or R&D team, care deeply about many issues other than the price of your product.

If you have analyzed the interests of all of the stakeholders in the organization affected by the purchasing decision, you can then determine whether their interests are in fact being satisfied by the buyer. If not, you can educate the buyer about this discrepancy and/or consider contacting those other stakeholders. If you have a strong enough relationship with the buyer, you might be able to partner with her in approaching other stakeholders in her organization to determine how their interests can be most effectively satisfied. If you have a weak or troubled relationship with the buyer, you may want to consider going around her to the other stakeholders. This is of course often a high risk strategy because by circumventing her, you are likely to damage your relationship with the buyer.

> *Your buyer may only care about price, but others in her organization care about many issues other than price!*

When you contact stakeholders other than the buyer, let them know how their critical interests on issues other than price may be harmed if their buyer considers only price. Also, encourage stakeholders within the account to let their buyer know how important issues other than price are to them. While you may be reluctant to alienate your buyer by going around her, you should weigh any potential harm to your relationship with her against the potential benefit you may obtain from building a coalition with other stakeholders in her organization not only on this deal but also in the future.

Strategy #3: Present the whole package.

On occasion, a buyer may try to force you to discuss price without allowing you to share information about how your proposal will satisfy a broader array of interests. For example, your buyer may set up a negotiation process that focuses first or last (or only) on price. When a buyer tries to force you into a "price negotiation" separate from the discussion of how your proposal will satisfy the overall interests of her organization, you should resist this. A negotiation focused on price alone is a trap!

> *You must show how your proposal will satisfy all of the critical interests of the buyer's organization.*

We saw in strategy #1 above how you can (and should) negotiate for an opportunity to wrap the price discussion into a broader conversation about what the account's critical interests are. Remember, you are not denying the importance of price to the buyer's decision. You are simply ensuring that the buyer's decision takes into account other factors in addition to price.

The difference between strategy #1 and strategy #3 is that here you will not merely confirm the critical interests of your buyer and her organization (as you did in strategy #1), but you must now show how your proposal will satisfy the critical interests of the buyer's organization. Treat it like a game of connecting the dots. Link each element of your proposal to the customer's critical needs that each element will satisfy. Do not leave anything to the imagination. Make it obvious. If appropriate, have a one or two page summary listing every element of the proposal of what is in the proposal and what critical customer needs each element of the proposal satisfies. Try to confirm with the buyer that the elements of your proposal satisfy her critical needs. If she disagrees, ask the buyer to help you understand what you are missing.

Strategy #4: Warn of consequences.

Okay, so you wondered whether we would get here. Perhaps you were itching to tell that buyer off. Maybe it's the last thing you want to do. After all, won't you lose the deal? And isn't that what buyers do: threaten sellers with consequences?! "I'm the seller!" you may point out. "It's not for me to warn of consequences. That's what buyers do!"

Yes, that's what buyers do. And it's also what savvy sellers do.

If you do not warn your buyer about the consequences of a bad decision—such as not buying your products and services—then you have missed one of your greatest opportunities to influence the buyer's decision-making in your favor. The idea here is not to threaten the buyer. Not at all. Instead, what you want to do is help your buyer make an informed decision by demonstrating how her organization's critical interests will be harmed if she does not agree to your proposal. Again, this is not a threat, but a calm, strategic conversation—best if supported by persuasive data—about the harm to the critical interests of the buyer's organization if you are unable to make a deal.

When done well, this *conversation about the consequences of not coming to agreement* actually makes it less likely that you will fail to come to agreement. I have been thanked by buyers for sharing this type of information! Why would they thank me? Because they had not thought about certain harms to their organization's critical interests if we failed to reach an agreement! When a deal appears sidetracked by price considerations, a frank discussion about the consequences of not coming to agreement can often provide the breakthrough you need to get the deal done.

> *Help your buyer make an informed decision by demonstrating how her organization's critical interests will be harmed if she does not agree to your proposal.*

The best way to have this conversation is in a professional, non-threatening, conversational tone. You don't want to be perceived by the buyer as desperate or mean-spirited, just helpful and well-informed. You <u>might</u> say something like, "I would have a concern if you went with that other offer because you would lose the benefit of our [element of my proposal—such as free technical support] that would really help you bring down your overall costs." The idea here is to link what might happen in the absence of a deal to the harm that would be changed to the critical needs of the buyer's organization.

Now, while you may not be absolutely sure about what will happen,[4] you are likely to be better prepared for this conversation than the buyer if you have done your homework and are aware of the impact of various possibilities on the critical interests of the buyer. The key here

---

[4] *What might happen in the event of no agreement is, by definition, the unknowable in the sense that you cannot be sure what every stakeholder will do in the absence of agreement. On the other hand, if you think it through carefully as a matter of risk analysis, you can get a pretty good idea of what people are likely to do. This is the information you can share with the buyer if you can establish that the buyer's organization will in fact be harmed by not agreeing to your proposal.*

is to communicate this information calmly and without rancor and then switch back to discussing the benefits of your proposed deal. That way, you can let the reality set in for your buyer: she is better off doing the deal with you.

Strategy #5: Reduce your package to meet the lower price.

Okay, we have only the fifth and final strategy remaining. And this one sounds an awful lot like caving in. How can you claim to be a successful, strategic sales negotiator if you agree to the buyer's price demands?! That's a fair question. The answer depends on your preparation and *what you agree to in addition to the price*. Here's how this works.

If at the end of the day your buyer will not budge from demanding a lower price than you have asked for in your proposed solution (for whatever reason), you have three options: 1) keep trying to get the buyer to go for a higher price; 2) walk away; or 3) accept the buyer's price. Let's look at each of these options.

> a. *Keep trying:* Strategies 1-4 above give you effective ways to influence the buyer's decision-making so as to avoid the price game. Before you give up on a deal (especially a potentially lucrative deal), you should try these strategies. But if after trying, you still cannot meet the buyer's price, then you should think carefully about whether your time is better spent

developing other opportunities than trying to squeeze blood out of this rock.

b. *Walk away:* The key here is to know when you are better off walking away than doing the deal. As noted above, there is a point of diminishing returns, when a deal is simply not worth doing.[5] In order to determine that bottom line/walk away point, you must carefully analyze the effects on your own interests (particularly your critical interests) if you walk away.

c. *Accept the buyer's price:* Wait a minute! Isn't the point here to avoid giving in on price?! And we're talking about accepting the buyer's lowball, unreasonable price? What gives?! Here it is. It can make sense to reduce your price if 1) you have done a strategic analysis of your interests in making this decision, and 2) you change your proposal to suit the lower price.

Here's what you do. Let's say your strategic analysis shows that your critical interests are better served by doing a deal even at your buyer's low price than by walking away. Okay, then you should do the deal. But what deal? Don't just agree to a lower price for the same proposal you had previously communicated. That would communicate to the buyer that you were trying to rip her off all along! And every future negotiation would start with the buyer assuming she could bring you down on price—the harder she bargained, the better. That would

---

[4] Your perspective on when this walk away point occurs often depends on your job function. For example, a financial analyst "supporting" the field may have a different view of the appropriate walk away point from a field sales rep, whose quota and livelihood depend on being able to close deals at almost any level as fast as possible.

make for a painful set of future interactions, as you tried to hold the line and she pushed to see how far you would go.

> *As a last resort, you may have to re-package the deal by removing certain elements from your proposal even though your buyer wants them and may have expected them to be included.*

Instead of merely giving in on price, then, re-package the deal by adjusting your previous proposal to suit the buyer's lower price. Make clear that certain elements of the previous proposal that your buyer may have expected will no longer be included. These elements could include product features, if applicable, and/or services. And clarify to the buyer that in your view this new, reduced proposal is inferior to your previous (recommended) proposal by showing which of her organization's critical interests will be less effectively satisfied—or even harmed—by the lower priced package. This preserves both your credibility and your value pricing for future negotiations with the buyer.

Those are the five key strategies for selling value when your buyer only wants to talk price. Remember to keep pushing back toward strategy #1 if you feel yourself slipping toward #5.

Common Mistakes:

The single most common mistake people make when faced with a hardball price negotiation is losing their cool, panicking and falling into the price game. Why does this happen? For a number of reasons. It can be caused by any of the following:

1. Seller's habit;
2. Buyer's expectation;
3. Seller's desperation; or
4. Powerful buyer.

Let's take a look at each type of challenge and how they lead to mistakes.

Seller's Habit: This is probably the most common mistake of all. The seller has simply gotten into the habit of leading with price, or discounts. This bad habit can be caused by a lack of training, a pervasive practice within an organization, or like most bad habits, people just sort of pick them up and do not know how to get rid of them. This bad habit of emphasizing price can be hard to break, particularly when you create customer expectations that this is how you sell (see Bad Habit #2 below). In other words, the more you emphasize price, rather than value, the more your customers think of you and your offerings in terms of price, not value.

The good news is that since the seller's behavior is driving the focus on price, the seller can change his behavior. With some training and guidance, even the most discount-addicted seller can turn it around and start selling value. I have seen many experienced sellers do it seemingly overnight. And best of all, when a seller achieves success by selling value, the new behavior is reinforced by that success and quickly replaces the old bad habit.

Buyer's Expectation: A close relative of Bad Habit #1, this one is not always the seller's fault. Sometimes a previous seller has encouraged the customer to think only of price. Or a competitor emphasizes price in order to compete against your offerings. Or a buyer may come from another context, such as another company or industry, in which she grew accustomed to thinking about price, not value.

In any of these situations, the key is to create new expectations for the buyer centering on value, not price in isolation. This is not easy to do. Under these circumstances, before you get into the five strategies listed above, you may have to address the buyer's expectations head on. You might say something like, "I appreciate that in our previous discussions, you and I have focused a lot on price. I know price is important to you. I also want to be sure I am understanding your organization's needs so that we can provide the most value to you possible. For that reason, I'd like to spend a moment making sure I understand your objectives." Of course, once you get that green light from the buyer, you go! You start with Strategy #1 above.

Seller's Desperation: Okay, so maybe it's a little cruel to go there. But let's face it, when the month or quarter is about to end and you need to close a deal to make your quota or stay out of a Performance

Improvement Plan, the temptation to play the price game is huge. That's why organizations have sales managers and finance departments, to put a check on this kind of behavior. But, again, in the real world, sales managers have their quotas as well, and finance can be circumvented or berated or just plain ignored. I think you get the point.

The temptation to lead with discounts or price can be great. And by giving in to temptation, many a good sales professional flirts with the dangers posed by Bad Habits #1 and #2. That is, what starts as a "one time" special offer becomes either the seller's habit or a new expectation of the buyer, or most often a mutually reinforcing combination of the two. How do you avoid temptation? It is simple, but not easy.

When we really want something—like closing a big deal when we are a little off our numbers, for example—we generally focus on our own needs. The key to avoiding the price game under these circumstances is to train ourselves to focus on how we can satisfy the buyer's needs in order to get our own needs met as part of closing the deal. This can be difficult to do and requires a good deal of practice and discipline. But it definitely can be done. And it is well worth the effort.

The Powerful Buyer: Look, it's easy to get confused about this one. So let's separate two ideas. Let's distinguish between 1) a buyer who is truly powerful because she has some kind of intrinsic leverage—say, her organization is the dominant player in its space and you have many strong competitors vying for its business; and 2) a buyer who appears powerful to you because she is good at playing the price game. While the two forms of power may go together, they often do not. That is, many powerful buyers are willing to consider your offer in terms of the total value you bring to their organizations. And many buyers who manipulate you into the price game do not actually enjoy any real leverage other than their ability to get you to play the game. So let's take each of the two aspects of a buyer's power in turn.

Genuine buying power is something you have to be aware of and take into account as you present your offer. In other words, do not pretend that things as significant as large volumes or aggressive competition are irrelevant to price. But just because they are relevant to price does not in and of itself mean that you should fall into the price game either. When you deal with a truly powerful buyer, be prepared to deal with price, but again do so in the context of the total value your offer can bring that powerful organization. Simply put, follow strategies 1-5 that we have discussed.

When dealing with the buyer who seems powerful because she is good at drawing you into the price game, you should prepare yourself to be tough. You may end up at Strategy #4 (educating your buyer about consequences) faster than you would like. But if you want to get out of the price game with a buyer who likes to play that game, you have to transform your interactions with the buyer into a conversation about value. Again, not easy, but it can be done.

Success Story:

An IT services company turns around a multi-million dollar deal that had bogged down on price.

An experienced account manager at an IT services company had hit the wall. To be precise, she had hit the price barrier. She needed the renewal of the account's contract, but the new buyer at the account said price was all that mattered. And when the buyer indicated that the price would have to <u>decrease</u>—not increase, as had been forecast for the account in the internal plan—the account manager was stuck.

So after consulting her manager, the account manager did what she always did in these situations. She went toe-to-toe with her finance department. And it was ugly. Finance would not give in. Both sides escalated the issue to senior managers. Now not only was a lot of money at stake, but internal relationships and the pricing structure of the company's offerings in the market were at stake as well. Given the strategic nature of the decision about how to proceed with the account, the account manager's boss requested that the account manager do an interests analysis to be sure that the company understood the critical interests of all stakeholders and had adequately considered options for satisfying those interests.

Though skeptical, the account manager realized she could not get authorization for the discount until she did an interests analysis. Partnering with an internal expert in interests analysis from the training department, the account manager identified the stakeholders at the account involved in or affected by the buying decision. The stakeholders included not only the buyer but also user groups, administrators and business leaders in the account's organization. The account manager did this in less than five minutes.

Next, the account manager identified issues that those stakeholders cared about relative to the buying decision. She figured this would be easy since all the buyer ever talked about was price. But the training department expert pushed back urging the account manager to consider what other stakeholders such as the user groups cared about. This yielded issues related to what content was included in the contract. When the training department expert asked what the administrators cared about, the account manager said there was nothing they cared about because the billing format was such a mess that they were recommending a competitor's solution. "They hate us," the account manager complained.

"Wait a minute!" the training department expert pointed out. "The administrators care about the <u>billing format</u>."

"Okay," the account manager agreed, not yet realizing the breakthrough.

"Well, it sounds like the administrators have a critical interest in improving the billing format. And that is something to talk about other than price!"

As the account manager and training department expert finished their interests analysis and began to brainstorm possible solutions that could satisfy the stakeholders' interests as part of an agreement, they got to that issue of the billing format. The account manager claimed nothing could be done about the billing format.

"Have you checked with our billing department?" the training department expert asked.

"What's the point?" the account manager objected. "They have their systems."

"Look, their interest may be to maintain a uniform system. But if it is not critical to them, maybe they will make an exception this time if it helps us close this deal."

Though still skeptical, the account manager checked with her contact in the billing department. She found out that some coding would have to be done, but that it was possible to change the billing format for this major account. "Just don't make a habit of it," the billing administrator warned. "Don't worry," the account manager explained, speaking to the billing department's interests. "We won't set a precedent here because this account has a unique issue with the billing format that we've never come across before."

With the possibility of solving the billing issue, the account manager contacted her buyer and requested a meeting with the buyer and the account's billing department. Although the buyer initially resisted, the account manager explained, "You know that problem your people have with our billing format? I think we may have a solution. And if it works as well as I think it will, your organization will save a lot of time and money. You'll be a hero!"

At the meeting, the account manager presented her possible solution on the billing format. The billing administrator was thrilled. **The buyer for the first time said nothing about price.** *Within a week, the contract renewal closed—with an <u>increase</u>, not a decrease—as a result of the company's flexibility in meeting the account's needs!*

When praised at the next divisional meeting as having performed a "miracle" in closing this major deal so fast and for an increase, the account manager credited the training department for helping her get it done. She said that by suggesting she look to other stakeholders, which uncovered this innovative billing solution, the training department had helped her defuse the price issue.

The entire preparation had taken two hours. The deal that closed was worth more than $5 million. And as important, the account perceived the deal as a bargain and subsequently purchased additional content!

Conclusion:

» There is no one "magic bullet" for the price game
» Use these five strategies in the order listed here
   1. Put price in a broader context
   2. Identify other stakeholders in the buyer's organization
   3. Present your whole package
   4. Educate the buyer about consequences
   5. Reduce your package to conform to a lower price, if necessary
» Communicate clearly to the buyer how your proposal will satisfy her critical needs
» Stay calm and strategic at all times even if you think you might lose the deal (live to fight another day)

CHAPTER **TWO**

Generating Consensus and Buy-in

with speed and flexibility

CHAPTER TWO
Generating Consensus and Buy-in
with speed and flexibility

The Challenge:

If everyone agreed all of the time, we wouldn't all be doing our jobs. On the other hand, a little consensus on objectives and strategy every now and then wouldn't be such a bad thing, would it?! The question is when does consensus make sense and when are people just caving in to avoid conflict? A related question is when should we cater to the whims of one difficult person (other than the CEO!) who refuses to get on board with a decision, perhaps just so he can say later, "I told you so?"

Over many years of working with various large organizations in different industries, I have come to realize that obtaining internal alignment on business objectives and strategy is often far more difficult than dealing with people outside the organization. This is because we tend to be more aware of and sensitive to the divergence of interests among internal stakeholders. After all, when it is internal, we have to deal with each other on an ongoing basis.

Our colleagues within the organization must perform a delicate balancing act. On the one hand, they must focus on their respective individual roles, whether finance or account management or product development; and on the other hand, they should at least consider the impact of their decisions on the organization as a whole. This is balancing act: often results in conflict, political gamesmanship, lost productivity, and frustration.

So the question is can we improve on the usual process of internal struggle without losing the valuable exchange of ideas and perspectives that creates tension but also often generates breakthroughs?

What we do when we're at our best:

What does success look like? It often takes the form of a structured framework for decision-making that is both efficient and evocative. Successful internal conversations solicit, even compel, honest exchanges of ideas about the organization's objectives *and the assumptions that drive those objectives*. The key is to include everyone relevant to the decision-making process without slowing the process itself.

Now, if this sounds unrealistic, I can assure you it is not. I have seen it happen many times. In fact, the alternatives—to move blithely ahead on strategic decisions without input from key stakeholders, or alternatively to bog down in a cumbersome process of trying to force consensus—are themselves fraught with peril. Why? Because I have seen time after time how a "great idea" in the executive suite flops upon implementation because either 1) some crucial aspect of the decision that would have surfaced had the field been consulted was missed, or

2) some obstructionist with a divergent (often inappropriate or hidden) agenda derails implementation.

So back to the fundamental question. What does it take to obtain internal buy-in and move forward expeditiously with a consensus decision? There are a number of factors.

> ## Keys to Obtaining Internal Buy-in:
>
> 1. Leadership must be transparent and neutral about the decision-making process.
> 2. The timing for a decision should be clear to everyone involved.
> 3. Everyone must understand which core interests will drive the decision-making process.
> 4. Any obstructionists must be neutralized.
> 5. Criteria for success should be clear to all involved.

First, leadership must be transparent about the decision-making process. That is, while leadership cannot guarantee any particular outcome, or that everyone will be equally satisfied by the outcome, the decision-making process should be inherently neutral and not skewed to any one stakeholder group's perspective.

Second, the timing for a decision should be communicated up front so that all stakeholders know how fast or deliberately the decision will be made. This eliminates confusion and game playing ("No one told me I had to get back to you by tomorrow!"). It also allows stakeholders to question the time frame if they believe it is inappropriately fast or slow. While the pursuit of consensus and the speed of decision-making may seem at first glance to be at odds with each other, this is not necessarily so. For example, a decision hastily made that lacks buy-in from key stakeholders is likely to take much longer to move forward (if in fact it ever moves forward) than a decision made through an efficient process that engages stakeholders and generates consensus.

Third, the key assumptions on which the decision will be based must be clarified and communicated in a transparent manner for all stakeholders. The key assumptions include 1) the interests of the organization as a whole; 2) the interests of internal stakeholders who may have different points of view (for example, the product development team when the organization is considering closing down an R&D facility); and 3) the interests of some external stakeholders, such as channel partners or customers. This means that the foundation on which decision-making is based will be robust enough to support effective implementation that includes a communication plan tailored to all affected stakeholders about how the decision will impact them and why the organization has chosen to move forward with the decision.

Fourth, if any team members have indicated that they do not support consensus decision-making, leadership should communicate that obstructionism will not be tolerated. Obstructionism generally takes the form of 1) a refusal to participate in the decision-making process and/or 2) a tendency to criticize the team's decisions after the fact (as though the obstructionist had not been consulted or involved in the decision-making). Both forms of obstructionism undermine the team, particularly if the obstructionist has the ear of senior leaders. It should therefore be addressed up front.

Finally, criteria for success should be built into the decision-making process as assumptions are evaluated and objectives confirmed. This allows both for ongoing engagement of stakeholders through implementation of the decision and for continuous improvement as unforeseen and better ideas surface. When the decision-making process itself generates buy-in from stakeholders, they are far more likely to see changes in strategy as being legitimate improvements than a failure of leadership to stick with a prescribed vision. This flexibility becomes mutually reinforcing when it is grounded in 1) a collective understanding of stakeholder interests and 2) a willingness to consider new options for satisfying those interests.

Common Mistakes:

While the benefits of consensus decision-making may seem obvious, if sometimes unattainable, there are sufficient pitfalls to require caution in pursuing buy-in and consensus from team members. Here are a few of the biggest mistakes.

First, never communicate that everyone should expect to be

equally happy with the outcome of important decisions. Not only is this unrealistic, it is actually undesirable. Each internal stakeholder has responsibility for his or her own function. The overall objective must be to satisfy as effectively as possible the critical interests of the entire organization—not to favor one faction over another or equalize outcomes across all functions.

Second, do not allow people's busy schedules to dictate the decision-making process. If the decision is important, then make sure the key stakeholders are engaged. If you need more time to get everyone together, arrange for that time or delay the decision. If you cannot delay the decision, communicate clearly to all key stakeholders that their input is requested and consider a variety of flexible ways (short of everyone being in the same room) to manage the decision-making process so as to maximize opportunities for buy-in and meaningful input.

Third, do not abandon the pursuit of consensus and buy-in when the going gets rough. Just because someone expresses doubts or disagreement with the emerging consensus of the team does not mean that that person should be either coddled (which encourages obstructionism) or ignored (the objector may, after all, be right). The appropriate way to handle objections is to require 1) that the objector explain the assumptions on which her objections are based, and 2) that other team members listen respectfully and ask clarifying questions, if appropriate. Once the assumptions underlying the objection have been clarified and evaluated, the discussion can continue as before, taking into account (if appropriate) any new information. By handling objections in this manner, we can manage interpersonal conflict and ensure that all relevant information is considered as part of the decision-making process. In sum, don't conflate dissatisfaction with the <u>outcome</u> of a transparent, disciplined decision-making process with dissatisfaction with the process itself.

John G. Shulman

Success Story:

Getting buy-in from a senior sales team in the transportation industry.

The experienced sales team at a large airline had strong relationships with key customers and stable revenue streams throughout the organization. The problem was that the company needed a new approach, shifting its sales emphasis from a general pursuit of all possible revenues to a targeted pursuit of higher-value revenues. The challenge was how to get such experienced, successful sales professionals to embrace this new approach so that the sales team could emphasize specific products and refocus channel partners and customers accordingly.

Senior members of the sales team expressed concern about and even disagreement with some aspects of the new approach. Without buy-in from key members of the sales team, there was a strong likelihood that the field would continue to sell the same products it had in the past. And to make matters worse, finance and marketing had already transitioned to the new initiative and were no longer as flexible as they had been in the past. Friction began to emerge between the field and headquarters. The field grew concerned about the impact of the initiative on some key channel partners and customers. Nonetheless, economic pressures in the industry made implementing the initiative an immediate priority for the company.

Working collaboratively with the sales leadership, the training department recognized that a framework had to be created to facilitate dialogue and sound decision-making among the disparate internal stakeholders. Consensus and buy-in from the field would be critical if the initiative were to get off the ground.
The training department and senior leadership partnered to sponsor a

Generating Consensus and Buy-in

facilitated group discussion. The format of the discussion enabled senior sales professionals to voice their concerns in a constructive manner and generated consensus between management and the field on how the company could align its business objectives more effectively with the interests of its channel partners and customers. Based on this discussion, members of management and the sales team developed an implementation plan to move the initiative forward in a manner that all key stakeholders, including some who were not present for the facilitated discussion, could support. In addition, the implementation plan specifically invited further analysis and dialogue on an ongoing basis among various functions within the organization to determine the effectiveness of the initiative and to coordinate messages to external partners and customers.

As a result of the process used for soliciting input and framing the discussion around key assumptions and business objectives of the organization, the initiative was not just accepted by the field; it was enthusiastically embraced. At the conclusion of the facilitated joint session with management, every internal stakeholder who had been involved felt aligned on the project and ready for implementation. The field started delivering on the initiative within days.

Months later, the team's momentum on implementation and continuous improvement of the initiative had not decreased. If anything, it had increased, as team members experienced success and connected more effectively with their channel partners, their customers and each other.

Conclusion:

» Consensus and buy-in are not impossible to achieve

» Balance time/efficiency vs. importance of the decision in deciding whom to include and how to accommodate participation

» Clarify and communicate a simple, transparent process for key decisions about which there is likely to be conflict

» Be as fast and efficient as possible without undermining the discipline and integrity of the decision-making process

» Include all key stakeholders in the process

» Focus on the interests of the organization as a whole, but take into account the interests of internal factions and external partners

» Do not allow any key stakeholders to undermine the process by claiming they were not invited to participate or by withholding their input

» Report key decisions in a manner that encourages flexibility and invites feedback for continuous improvement

CHAPTER **THREE**

Handling Difficult People

without losing sleep or your shirt

CHAPTER THREE
Handling Difficult People
without losing sleep or your shirt

The Challenge:

I deal with a lot of difficult people. In my work as a negotiator, I often get called in to stop a bully who has been tormenting an organization. As a lawyer, I have dealt with obnoxious lawyers, power-hungry bureaucrats and self-proclaimed "alpha males." You know the type. They love dishing it out. But they can rarely take it when you hit back, especially when you hit them where it hurts—their critical interests.

But we're getting ahead of ourselves. Before we get into how to deal with difficult people, let's understand who these people are that drive us crazy. They pop up in all sorts of places. They can be our bosses, our co-workers, our neighbors and family. They are bullies who cannot tolerate anything short of domination. They torment you. They berate you. They refuse to be reasonable. They treat every discussion as a battle of wills. They yell, they shame, they just say, "No!" They take pleasure in depriving you of what you need. They are *difficult people who want to dominate you and are prepared to use a variety of tactics to get their way.*

I think you know who we are talking about. We all have a few of them in our lives. And if we had a way to handle them effectively, our lives would be much more harmonious and enjoyable. So let's look at how it's done.

What we do when we're at our best:

If you have read the earlier section on how to sell value when your buyer only wants to talk price, you'll find that we're going to cover some of the same ground here. Why would we do so? Two reasons: 1) a bully and a difficult buyer often rely on similar tactics; and 2) the ability to stay calm and strategic requires a lot of practice.

I'll use myself as an example. Even after years of working on the ideas presented here and negotiating high stakes deals with difficult people and in difficult situations, I find that I need to remind myself to stay calm and be strategic, especially when I really want a good result or when I'm tempted to lash back at a bully. Why is this so difficult? First of all, most bullies have it coming. And it sure feels good in the moment to hit a bully where it hurts. But as soon as you react in the heat of the moment, the bully knows he is winning. He is controlling our interaction by compelling me to react to his provocations. So we'll start once again by taking a deep breath and avoid reacting in the heat of the moment.

Now it's easy for me to write this. And it may even make sense as you read it. But the truth of the matter is that in the heat of the moment, it is not so easy to take that deep breath and refuse to react to a bully's provocations. In fact, it requires extraordinary emotional control and confidence not to react, which is why it is necessary. You see, when a difficult person provokes you, he wants you to react. He wants to precipitate your interactions so that you are not in control; he is. Then he can influence the outcome of the negotiation in a manner favorable to him. That is his game. Make no mistake, this is a bully's game, and it is generally not irrational behavior you are dealing with, even when you think it is.[6]

You do not want to play the bully's game. Not because you are weak or afraid, but because you do not need to waste your time and energy in such games. **Moreover, the more you indulge in back and forth exchanges with a difficult person, the less likely you are to get what you want.** It is a profoundly inefficient and ineffective way to deal with a difficult person.

So what do you do? You stay calm and think strategically. Again easy to write here. Hard to do when the stakes are high. What do I mean by being strategic? **Always ask yourself the following question:** *For*

---

[6] *We often indulge in the fantasy that those with whom we have conflict are "irrational." This is a common conceit that makes us feel better about our inability to move conversations forward or improve troubled relationships. It is not generally an accurate assessment of the other person, however. How do I know this? Because I have been in the crucible of profound, prolonged conflict in "hot spots" around the globe. Whether participating on a team facilitating dialogue among Israeli leaders over the withdrawal of settlements from Gaza and the West Bank, or mediating labor disputes in Asia and the United States, or negotiating the resolution of business disputes in numerous industries, I have yet to come across the truly irrational negotiator.*

John G. Shulman

what purpose?

Okay, what does that mean? I'll explain. Many times I have been called on to assist with a negotiation that is underway or is framed by a pre-existing, troubled relationship. Maybe there have been a series of unproductive interactions. Or there is reason to believe that the parties have reached impasse. What happens at this point? There is little, if any, trust between the parties (often for good reason). And small things start taking on greater and greater significance.

When I say "small things," what do I mean? In the context of negotiating a deal worth hundreds of millions of dollars, you find senior executives digging in over things like who goes first at the next meeting. Or where the meeting should take place. Or who should be there. Or when the meeting should take place. Now I don't mean to suggest that these things are irrelevant. But we should consider these minor issues in a broader context.

What is that context? It is with an understanding of how each issue

---

Okay, I take that back. When I get home from one of these trips, I encounter my young children. And I will say that up to about age 5, the concepts of cause and effect tend to be overwhelmed often by waves of irresistible emotion.

But the real point here is that while you may deal with difficult people and emotional people, in my experience you generally don't deal with irrational people, especially in a business context. You may not agree with the other person's views or value system, but I think you will find that even a person with whom you fundamentally disagree will still try to satisfy his interests, including those interests that appear to you to be profoundly irrational.

relates to our ability to satisfy our interests. In other words, before we make a stink about where the negotiation should take place or who will be there, we should ask *why it matters!* **We should ask the question, "For what purpose?"**

Rather than make important decisions because our senior executive wants to prove he is "tougher" than the executive on the other side, we should **drive our decision-making and behavior** in a manner calibrated to satisfy our organization's critical interests as effectively as possible.

And how do we do that? There is a simple three step approach that can help you stay strategic and get what you want, even when you are dealing with a particularly difficult negotiator. So let's go through three simple steps that will keep you strategic and out of the bully's game.

Handling Difficult People

Step 1: *Stay Strategic by Focusing on Interests*

Step 2: *Propose Options for Satisfying Each Other's Interests*

Step 3: *First Understand, Then if Necessary, Communicate Consequences to the Difficult Person*

Step 1: Stay Strategic by Focusing on Interests

Know your interests, or needs. This step is critical but often overlooked, particularly when you are in the heat of battle with a difficult person who keeps trying to provoke you into a reaction. When that antagonist attacks you, refuses to acknowledge your perspective, belittles you, ignores you, or engages in any number of similar tactics designed to prevent you from being strategic, you should step back, take a deep breath, and ask yourself as you consider your next action, "*For what purpose?*" In other words, how will my next move satisfy or harm my interests? While this sounds easy, it is not.

Difficult people know that the vast majority of people is unable to remain strategic when attacked. **In fact, when attacked, most people don't think—they react!**

When attacked by a difficult adversary, most people either fight back reflexively—driven by a desire to defend themselves—or retreat and capitulate. The difficult person attacks in order to force you into one of those two responses. In this manner, the attacker controls the situation and controls you.

But you need not fall into the trap. There is a better way.

When you are attacked, it is essential that you choose not to react in the heat of the moment to the provocation!

Now this does not mean you are scared or unable to fight back.

Quite to the contrary; it means that you will impose consequences for bad behavior not in an emotional, heat of the moment reaction, but in a cold, calculating, strategic manner. You will determine how best to satisfy your own interests or harm your adversary's interests, or if possible, do both. In order to do so, you must remain calm, composed and firm even when the other person gets out of control.

This does not mean you should tolerate unprofessional or inappropriate behavior from others. It means you will communicate in a firm, unemotional manner that such behavior is unacceptable and will not be tolerated.

Once you have established ground rules of professional, respectful behavior, it is time to explore whether there is any realistic possibility of satisfying each other's interests.

You want to satisfy your own interests and, to the extent you can, satisfy the legitimate interests of the difficult person. This is an important point. Unless you are able to satisfy the legitimate interests of that difficult person, you should not expect him to agree to anything that you want! This leads us to step 2.

Step 2: Propose Options for Satisfying Each Other's Interests

Once you have a clear understanding of your own interests and the legitimate interests of the difficult person, explore options for satisfying those interests. If your adversary won't participate in collaborative problem-solving, do the following exercise on your own:

Exercise: Make a list of your interests. **Circle those interests of yours that are critical to you.** Next, make a list of the difficult person's interests, including illegitimate interests like intimidating you. **Circle only the legitimate interests of your adversary.** Finally, think of every possible action you or the difficult person could take as part of a negotiated agreement that could satisfy a) your interests, b) your adversary's legitimate interests, and/or c) both of your interests.

The worksheet on the next page provides a framework for doing this exercise.

Handling Difficult People

The Alignor® Process Worksheet

Step 1: Identify People's NEEDS:

PERSON:	
NEEDS:	

Step 2: Brainstorm Possible ACTIONS:

Now you have a list of possible actions from which you can craft a proposal for a negotiated resolution with the difficult person. Start by grouping possible actions into the following three categories:

1. Actions you would like to do or discuss as part of a negotiated agreement because they are either a) high value to you, or b) high value to your adversary and low cost to you;
2. Actions you are willing to consider as part of a negotiated agreement; and
3. Actions you are NOT willing to consider under any circumstances.

As you consider which actions to place in each category, try to avoid putting actions into category 3 since you want to maintain your flexibility as you consider various packages of actions. Similarly, just because you put a given action into the first category does not mean you will necessarily agree to it. The idea at this stage is to preserve as much flexibility as possible for exploring options that will satisfy your interests and, to the extent possible, will also satisfy the interests of the difficult person.

Before you finalize a proposal, you have more work to do. You must think about the possible "fighting alternatives" that may occur if you do not come to agreement. In other words, you must figure out what is reasonable to offer and expect in return based on the leverage you have and the leverage your adversary will have if you do not come to agreement. For example, **if you do not negotiate an agreement, will you be able to satisfy your critical interests unilaterally or harm**

your adversary's critical interests? Will the difficult person be able to satisfy his own critical interests unilaterally or harm your critical interests if there is no agreement? We are now ready for step 3.

Step 3: First Understand, Then if Necessary, Communicate Consequences to the Difficult Person

While you may hope to avoid this step by doing a good job coming up with attractive proposals in step 2 above, you must keep in mind that you are dealing with a difficult person. This means you may have to communicate or even impose consequences in order to keep negotiations on track. A difficult person will often refuse to be reasonable as a tactic to see if you will cave in and concede more. Therefore, even if you are creative and fair, and you propose wonderful solutions that will satisfy your adversary's legitimate interests, that person may—out of habit or spite—test you to see if you are weak or foolish or holding back additional value that might be extracted through pressure tactics.

For this reason, and as a matter of sound decision-making to determine how much leverage you have with the difficult person, you should evaluate what might happen in the absence of an agreement. We call these possibilities "fighting alternatives." What are fighting alternatives? **Fighting alternatives are the things people may do to satisfy their own interests unilaterally, and to harm the interests of others in the absence of a negotiated agreement.**[7]

For example, if your adversary will be better off not agreeing to what you want, then you need to know that. Or, by contrast, if your adversary will be worse off by not coming to agreement with you than by accepting what you are prepared to propose, then you need to know that—and probably educate him about it as well. This analysis is commonly referred to as "leverage."

Implementation

Once you have an understanding as to what may happen if you and your adversary do not come to agreement, the next step is to go back to your list of possible actions and refine it further into a best case proposal. Put that package of actions into a proposal or talking points that can be communicated to your adversary. A format that is particularly effective and persuasive is to:

---

[7] *The phrase "fighting alternatives" may seem unnecessarily provocative. Indeed, in his seminal book Getting to Yes, Roger Fisher refers to "Best Alternative to Negotiated Agreement" (or "BATNA") as the outcome if you do not reach a negotiated agreement. While "fighting alternatives" is similar to "BATNA," I have found that in the real world the absence of a negotiated agreement means more than just people trying to satisfy their own interests unilaterally. The absence of a negotiated agreement—particularly when you are dealing with difficult people—often means conflict! And conflict means people impose consequences against their perceived adversaries even when those imposing the consequences do not themselves benefit from the consequences. They do it out of anger or perhaps a sense that the consequences will soften up their adversary in the future. So even though the phrase "fighting alternatives" may seem harsh, I find it useful as a reminder that in the real world the absence of a negotiated agreement can mean damaging conflict—conflict that damages relationships and substantive interests.*

- » **Identify the interests of your adversary that will be satisfied by your proposal**
- » **Link the specific actions in your proposal that will satisfy the identified actions**
- » **Express flexibility if your adversary has other ideas as to how those interests might be satisfied more effectively by modifying your proposal** *without harming your interests.*

Invite a conversation about both the specific actions in your proposal and why you believe they will satisfy your counterpart's interests. A difficult person will often challenge your assumptions about how effectively his interests will be satisfied (and may not care whether your interests are satisfied or harmed). That conversation, as tough as it may be, is still preferable to the games difficult people like to get you to play!

And what if your adversary persists with bad behavior or refuses to accept your proposal even though it satisfies his interests? In the real world, this happens. You must then be prepared to communicate or even impose consequences. You should communicate this information about consequences in a calm, strategic manner. The most effective way to do this is to:

Explain (in a respectful manner) the harm to your adversary's interests that will occur if you do not come to agreement and you are forced to impose fighting alternatives.

Of course, this can be a difficult conversation. For example, your adversary may feel that you are threatening him. It is therefore essential that even as you communicate what may sound like threats, you do so in a calm, unemotional manner and emphasize how you would prefer to get back to a discussion of negotiation options that could satisfy your interests and the interests of your adversary. In short, you hold in one hand a package of carrots (your negotiation proposal) and in your other hand, the sticks (fighting alternatives).

This approach will generally maximize your chances of coming to a negotiated agreement. On occasion, it will result in your concluding that you are better off pursuing "fighting alternatives," and you will walk away from a deal. What is significant, though, is that you use a disciplined approach to handling your adversary. This enables you to resist the knee-jerk reactions that your adversary may try to elicit from you so as to gain control of the situation. When you are able to stay strategic, you maximize your chances of satisfying your critical interests. And that is a great outcome when you are dealing with a difficult person—or anyone else for that matter.

Common Mistakes:

The most common mistake we make is not recognizing tactics for what they are: an attempt by a difficult person to throw us off, make us less strategic and control the interaction. In short, we fall into the trap of merely reacting—often in anger or outrage or frustration—to provocations that are intended to make us do just that! Instead, when we recognize our adversary's games and tactics, if we take a deep breath and remain strategic, we can defuse the tactics and games by <u>not</u> reacting. It is as simple (though not easy, in the heat of the moment) as that.

Another common mistake is when we assume that just because someone says things with which we disagree that he is crazy or irrational. The difference in our perspectives may come from a number of things. It may come from divergent assumptions we are making based on our respective experiences. It may come from incompatible views we have developed about how to deal with conflict, people, or certain types of interactions. For example, I may believe in holding back information when I perceive conflict and you may be inclined to share information in the hope of averting conflict.

And different perspectives most often come from our unique individual biases about what our needs are and how we can best satisfy those needs. Some of us are more prone to building relationships that we believe will enable us to get what we need long term. Others take the view that it is a "dog-eat-dog" world out there in which everyone must protect himself and get what he can whenever he can—the "buyer beware" kind of approach. These divergent approaches often yield differences in views and actions so fundamental that we become tempted to view the other person as not merely different from ourselves, but actually as the irrational person of our nightmares!

So the next time you are tempted to dismiss the difficult person you are dealing with as "irrational," explore whether there are differences in perspectives, needs and experiences that may be driving the behavior you deem irrational. Figure out the assumptions your adversary is making about her needs. Then see if there are ways to satisfy those needs as part of an agreement, even if you do not necessarily agree with or completely understand those needs. (After all, they are not your needs!) And remember, just because you explore options for satisfying your adversary's apparent needs does not mean you will necessarily agree to those options. You need only satisfy your adversary's needs as part of an agreement if by doing so you will more effectively satisfy your own needs than you would if you were not to come to an agreement.

One other common mistake we often make when dealing with difficult people is we assume that our adversary will always be difficult no matter what we do. This is an important point. Human beings are social animals. We respond to other humans and to the contexts in which we find ourselves. Thus, if you persist in urging a collaborative, problem-solving approach to your interactions with even a difficult person who habitually creates conflict and discord, you may find over time that the context you create will change that person's behavior. Best case, you may even convert an adversary into an ally.

Handling Difficult People

Success Story:

I knew Fred was going to be trouble as soon as I entered the room. He strolled over to shake my hand and communicate to his subordinates that I was his guy. It was obvious that Fred was in control and planned to keep it that way. As soon as he had ushered me to a spot at the conference table, Fred told his team that Amy, the president of the company, had suggested I could help the team handle a troublesome competitor/partner. "It seems," Fred told the group, "that Amy thinks John can help us deal with our Canadian friends." After a pause for dramatic effect, Fred snorted, "I say you people just have to learn to say, 'No.'"

The other members of the team looked to me for a reaction. They had worked with me on previous deals and knew they could count on me to bring a transparent, disciplined, process-driven approach to the negotiation. They thought of me as the "win-win" interest-based negotiation guy. And they had told me when I agreed to take on this assignment that Fred was driving the organization over a cliff, blindfolded.

So what I said next caught them off guard and caused dismay. "Why stop at 'No?'" I pressed Fred. "That would be letting the Canadians off easy. Why not attack them with everything we've got? Really hit them hard!"

Fred was stunned. He hadn't thought of that. The others in the room were stunned. They had counted on me to curb Fred's worst impulses, not encourage or even top them. "Let's do it," Fred agreed, having found in me a new best friend.

So we analyzed first the interests of our organization and then looked at the interests of the Canadian partner/competitor. Once we had done this interests analysis, we jumped past Step 2, in which we should have brainstormed possible actions for a negotiated agreement, and went straight to Step 3: fighting alternatives!

Fred was ecstatic. He reveled in the very name of Step 3. "Fighting alternatives," he said, rolling it off his tongue and savoring the flavor, and the distress it caused the "wimps" on his team. He appeared giddy as we outlined all the things we could do to attack the interests of the partner/ competitor. The others in the room grew queasy. Then, just as Fred declared that this was the best process he had ever seen for preparing for battle, I cautioned, "Wait, we're not done!"

Fred said he had all he needed and thanked me for my work. He got up to leave.

"No," I insisted. "We're not done."

Fred sat down. The others in the room held their breath, waiting to see what would happen next. They began to suspect this would be good.

"Let's turn it around," I suggested.

"What do you mean?" Fred asked.

"Well, you didn't think we'd be the only ones to pursue fighting alternatives if things don't work out, did you?" I pressed Fred.

"Well…" Fred paused. He realized for the first time that he was trapped. And he knew I had led him there. But he still didn't know how bad it would be.

I was aware that Fred had driven his team members to the verge of quitting. It was time to deliver a lesson that Fred would never forget. And it would be

Handling Difficult People

delivered in front of the entire team.

"Let's look at what the Canadians will likely do," I insisted. And so we did. And it was ugly. And the further we took the analysis, the more emphatically various team members pointed out that many of these 'fighting alternatives' were already being implemented in the market—with disastrous consequences for us!

As we laid out the litany of horrors, it became clearer and clearer that Fred had been the junior varsity fighting against the varsity with one arm tied behind his back. In fact, it turned out the Canadians had become so embarrassed by the one-sided nature of the battle that they were contacting people in our organization to find out who had hit Fred with an idiot stick.

When the meeting ended, Fred thanked me and ushered me out. He called me the next day and told me that he thought our process was great but that his team wasn't ready for it. He asked whether I could work with him privately on the side. I declined.

Within a month of the meeting, Fred was gone. It seems Amy had looked at our analysis—over Fred's objections—and realized that what her team needed was not someone who could just say "no," but a new leader who could actually think through the consequences of conflict in advance so that the entire organization would not have to be hit upside the head to realize fighting can hurt.

And once Fred was gone, Amy's organization did indeed re-engage the troublesome Canadians. But this time, the team was prepared, all team members were aligned and clear about the strategy and their roles, and the outcome was favorable. Fred was not invited back for the victory party.

Conclusion:

» Stay calm and strategic

» Understand that your adversary's game is to throw you off and keep you from being strategic

» Try to understand your adversary's critical interests, including illegitimate interests that may drive his decision-making

» Brainstorm options for satisfying your adversary's legitimate interests

» Understand what you can do to satisfy your own interests and, if appropriate, harm the critical interests of your adversary if there is no agreement

» Understand what your adversary may do to you in the absence of an agreement

» Propose a solution that satisfies the interests of your adversary to the best of your ability

» Be prepared to communicate and, if necessary, implement "fighting alternative"

» It bears repeating: remain calm and strategic![8]

---

[8] *Especially when he yells at you! Good luck dealing with those bullies. And feel free to contact me at jshulman@alignor.com.*

About the Author

John G. Shulman is an experienced attorney, negotiator, entrepreneur and public speaker skilled in the art and science of interest-based negotiation. With an A.B. in English from Harvard College and a J.D. from Harvard Law School, Mr. Shulman trained with leaders in the negotiation field. Mr. Shulman has worked with the Harvard Program on Negotiation on a project in the Middle East addressing conflict over Gaza and the West Bank. He has provided negotiation and conflict resolution training to United Nations personnel at the War Crimes Tribunal for Rwanda. Mr. Shulman is also a founder of the Center for Negotiation and Justice at William Mitchell College of Law in Minnesota and is a Visiting Professor of Law at the National Law University, Delhi, India.

Mr. Shulman has employed advanced interest-based strategies with a wide variety of clients, including 3M, ABN AMRO Bank, AstraZeneca, Blue Cross Blue Shield, the CCIM Institute, Delta Air Lines, Disney, General Mills, the Government of India, HealthPartners, Imation, International Dairy Queen, the Municipality of Dubai, Mylan Pharmaceuticals, PanAmSat, Sandoz Pharmaceuticals, Schwan's, Syngenta, Thomson Reuters, US Bank, Xcel Energy, the United Nations, and the US State Department and GSA.

In 1999, Mr. Shulman and colleagues with negotiation expertise founded Alignor to assist organizations in implementing an interest-based approach to decision-making and negotiation. Alignor's approach is currently used by several large organizations, including Imation Corp., which awarded Mr. Shulman its prestigious "Chairman's Business Turning Point Award" in 2002.

Mr. Shulman has conducted seminars and training workshops for thousands of business leaders and managers, judges, attorneys, commercial real estate professionals, government officials and community leaders in interest-based approaches to negotiation, assertiveness, influencing, collaboration, sales, account management, supply chain management, leadership, strategic thinking, and conflict resolution.

Along with one of the co-founders of Alignor, Mr. Shulman wrote and directed the critically acclaimed human rights movie 'JUSTICE.'

Along with one of the co-founders of Alignor, Mr. Shulman wrote and directed the critically acclaimed human rights movie 'JUSTICE.' Mr. Shulman wrote the children's fantasy novel, "The Lama, the Snow Leopard and the Thunder Dragon," published by Hachette. He has also played professional soccer in Asia and has traveled to and negotiated in over forty countries around the world.

About Alignor

Alignor is the global leader in performance improvement solutions utilizing the interest-based approach to negotiation, assertiveness, influencing, collaboration, sales, conflict resolution and leadership development. Alignor was founded by Harvard graduates and expert negotiators who developed a streamlined, effective approach to collaborating across functions, managing negotiations, handling business challenges and resolving disputes. Alignor helps its clients achieve their business objectives through a wide array of products and services, including customized training, expert coaching and consulting, scenario-based interactive simulations, blended learning and e-learning, evaluation tools, and customized job aids.

The Alignor approach to negotiation, assertiveness, influencing, collaboration, sales, and leadership development has been embraced by clients in numerous industries as a "best practice" for such core activities as project management, account management, sales, contract negotiations, mergers and acquisitions, strategic decisions, supply chain management, conflict resolution, customer service and improving organizational alignment.

Organizations implementing Alignor's approach to collaboration, assertiveness, influencing, project management, negotiation, sales, and leadership development have documented substantial revenue increases, faster closing time for deals, reduced costs, less conflict, more collaboration and stronger relationships (internal and external) that they attribute to their work with Alignor.

Alignor has trained and worked with thousands of business managers and leaders, professionals, lawyers, judges, community leaders and government officials from organizations throughout India, the United States and the world, including 3M, ABN AMRO, AstraZeneca, Bank of Bahrain and Kuwait, Blue Cross Blue Shield, Cadbury, CCIM Institute, Cummins, Delta Air Lines, Disney, General Mills, Government of India, Grupo Televisa, HealthPartners, High Courts of various states in India, Imation Corp, International Dairy Queen, Municipality of Dubai, Mylan Pharmaceuticals, PanAmSat, Pepsico, Polaroid, Sandoz Pharmaceuticals, Schwan's, SuperValu, Syngenta, the United Nations, US Bank, United States Government, US Department of State, and Xcel Energy.

Alignor works with clients on collaboration, assertiveness, influencing, negotiation, sales, project management, supply chain management, and leadership strategy and implementation, and has negotiated agreements in the health care, transportation, food, manufacturing, commercial real estate, high tech, financial services, legal services, and entertainment industries, among others. Alignor's work includes partnering with the Harvard Program on Negotiation to facilitate dialogue in the Middle East concerning Gaza and the West

About Alignor

Bank and training personnel at the UN War Crimes Tribunal for Rwanda. Alignor also provides workshops to lawyers, judges, community advocates and leaders in the United States, India, Africa and across Asia in negotiation, empowerment, and conflict resolution strategies. In India, Alignor has partnered with the National Law University, Delhi, the National Institute of Rural Development, Hyderabad, and the National Council of Rural Institutes, Hyderabad, to bring world class training and consulting services to the legal, corporate, government and NGO sectors.